D0189267

JOANNE LIMBURG

Bookside Down

Joanne Limburg published her first poetry collection, *Femenismo*, in 2000. Since then she has published one more full collection, one pamphlet and a prose memoir, *The Woman Who Thought Too Much*. She lives in Cambridge with her husband and son, who told her it was high time she wrote some poetry for him.

Also by Joanne Limburg

POETRY FOR ADULTS

Femenismo

Paraphernalia

The Oxygen Man

MEMOIR

The Woman Who Thought Too Much

JOANNE LIMBURG

Bookside Down

Cromer

PUBLISHED BY SALT
12 Norwich Road, Cromer, Norfolk NR27 0AX
United Kingdom

First published 2013

Printed in the UK by TJ International Ltd, Padstow, Cornwall

Typeset in Oneleigh 11/14

ISBN 978 1 907773 52 5 paperback

1 3 5 7 9 8 6 4 2

For Ivo and Chloe

CONTENTS

ACKNOWLEDGEMENTS

Thanks are due to my son and to other readers from 4L/5F, to my agent Louise and husband Chris and to Michelle McGrane, who published three of these poems on her website, Peony Moon.

THE OTHER SIDE OF THE SUN

What my mum doesn't know is
I have my own planet.

You can't see it from the earth:
it's the other side of the sun,
and everything there is opposite:

they go to bed in the morning,
and they get up at night,

the children teach the grown-ups
and tell them off at home,

the best food there is crisps
and broccoli is bad- very bad.

In Otherside language,
'You poo!' means 'I love you!',

showing your bottom
is waving politely

and if you blow a raspberry,
right in your mum's face, or your dad's,
and accidentally spit on them,

well then, you're really kissing them,
but in the Otherside way.

WHO CHASES WHO

Ben chases Esme,
and she chases Max;
Max waits for Lily,
and then he attacks;

Lily likes Matthew,
but Lily is shy,
so Emily grabs him
while Lily stands by,

but sometimes she's too busy
running from Fred,
whose Mia's fiancé—
or so Mia *said*—

though it's Thomas who chases her
during big play,
when he's not dodging Ruby
who kissed him one day,

after Oliver caught her;
now Sophie's got him,
and Tim's after Sophie,
and Skye's chasing Tim,

and Sam chases Skye

and Grace chases Sam
and George chases Grace
and I'm hiding, I am.

THE FEELING OF HAVING A GOOD DAY

Hallelujah —
I'm awake!
This day belongs to me

and I'm its favourite.
It wants to lick me
like a dog.

The world
is a balloon
that's on my string.

I'll get a prize
at school assembly
for being me,

then all the lessons
will be about
my awesomeness

and at break
I'll kick the football
to Australia.

I can see it in the mirror
when I smile—
I have electric teeth!

BEWARE THE HUMANS

So terrible humans are, hideous, cruel,
they are nightmares with nostrils,
disasters in shoes,
shrieking in daytime, rasping by moonlight,
loud as astonishment, stupid as glue.

O beware humans, see them and shun them,
they breath rotten eggs
and they wear stolen skins,
they quarrel in daylight, and dribble at night time,
vicious as triangles, madder than pears.

Observe now the human, hiccupping, sneezing,
squeezing dead cow
through a hole in his face,
he slobbers in daytime, his guts groan by moonlight,
slimy as six o'clock, rude as a boot.

Such are the humans then, horrible, pitiful,
tail-less absurdities,
ruthless mistakes
that gibber in daylight, and whimper at night time,
lost as last Wednesday, and sadder than soup.

THE DINOSAURS DIED

The dinosaurs died because they fell into a volcano
The dinosaurs died because they couldn't swim
The dinosaurs died because they got eaten by cave-men
The dinosaurs died because the Anglo-Saxons gave them
 chicken pox

And the dinosaurs died because because
And the dinosaurs died because

The dinosaurs died because they never washed
The dinosaurs died because seeds turned to trees in their
 tummies
The dinosaurs died because the mammals came along and
 wouldn't share
The dinosaurs died because they were mind-zapped by aliens

And the dinosaurs died because because
And the dinosaurs died because

The dinosaurs died because they dissolved
The dinosaurs died because they ran out of crisps
The dinosaurs died because they were eaten by giant
 cockroaches
The dinosaurs died because of their unacceptable behaviour

And the dinosaurs died because because
And the dinosaurs died because

The dinosaurs died because they were rude
The dinosaurs died because they didn't look where they were
going
The dinosaurs died because of bad television
The dinosaurs died because Victorians ran them over on their
penny-farthings

And the dinosaurs died because because
And the dinosaurs died because

The dinosaurs died because they didn't listen
The dinosaurs died because there was a lot of it about and they
all caught it
The dinosaurs died because insects crawled into their ears and
ate their brains
The dinosaurs died because they forgot to save

And the dinosaurs died — it's really true
And the dinosaurs died — they did, you know
And the dinosaurs died because because
And the dinosaurs died because

BANANAPHONE

for Max and Katya

At lunch today
my sister called me up on her banana.

I picked up mine and said, 'Hello?'
She just said 'Sorry?'

I said, 'Hello again. It's me. How's lunch?'
She said 'Sorry?' twice,

then she held her banana at arm's length,
and frowned at it,
then put it back against her ear,
so I tried 'How's lunch?' again

but she just shook her head.
She said, 'You're breaking up, I can't quite —
hang on a minute — '

She moved her chair right next mine,
so I asked, 'Better now?'

My sister wrinkled up her nose. She tutted.
'The reception on this phone,' she said,
'is terrible. You know what the trouble is?'

'No network coverage?' I asked.

'No,' she said. 'I'm guessing it's not ripe
enough.'

BOOKSIDE DOWN

Never read a book standing on your head, they said.
I asked why. They said, *Just don't*, so I did.

I went into my room, I took *Bob Beats the Baddies*
off the shelf, and then I turned us bookside down.

The book was open at my favourite picture,
the one with the baddies caught up in Bob's trap,

all open mouths with words coming out like 'Help!'
and 'Aaagh!'. They look so stupid. It's funny.

And it was just as funny bookside down, at first —
until the funny started turning into strange.

Right side up, you see, Bob had all the baddies
hanging from the ceiling, but bookside down,

the ceiling was the floor, so all the baddies
landed on it, and untied themselves.

Meanwhile Bob, his dog, and his friend Nancy
were standing on the floor, but bookside down,

the floor became the ceiling, so they fell off it,
and went thumping down headfirst,

and there they lay, stars and birds of dizziness
all fluttering and popping round their heads.

Then, bookside down, the baddies came,
and, bookside down, they took the ropes

and tied the friends and then — they WON!
Now that was WRONG, so straightaway

I jumped back on my feet, and shut the book.
For a moment then I stood, not looking

at the book still in my hand. Not looking,
scared I'd turned it bookside down forever.

Still not looking, I put it on the shelf.
Still not looking, I walked to the door

- but then I had a look: *Bob Beats The Baddies*,
the title said, and in my favourite picture,

the baddies and Bob were bookside back.
I think I got away with it that time. Don't tell.

YES-MAN

Dad, Dad, is this my lunch?
Yes.
And are you having your lunch too?
Yes.
And are we going out after lunch?
Yes.
Are we going into town after lunch?
Yes.
And are we going on the bus?
Yes.
And can I have my pocket money?
Yes.
And can I buy a comic with my pocket money?
Yes.
And can we take the bus back?
Yes.
And can I ask you something else?
Yes.
Will you always say yes now?
No.

COMPUTAPETS

Mum doesn't understand why I'm so upset.
She's doesn't know what it means to have a computapet,

that you have to go online at least once a day
to check on them, so they don't get sad or starve or run
away

because they don't feel loved or worst of all, just sort of *fade*
like they do when you haven't fed them yummichocs or
peppyade

and she doesn't even realise you have to buy that stuff
which you can't do if you haven't earned enough

and the only way to get the coins is to play Whoosajit and
win
and I can't even play a single game if she won't let me log
in.

Then Mum says, *But what is it that you're crying for?*
So they run away — well then you get some more,

they all look very much the same to me.
But if Mum had a proper look, she'd see

that every one's unique: some sleep a lot, and some are

greedy,
some really like a certain food, some are naughty, some
are needy —

they follow you about, and if you don't play with them
they cry.
I should be checking on them now. It's her fault if they
die.

AND THEN MY BROTHER SAID

So we were just leaving the house,
and I said
Wait! There's something in my shoe.
and then my brother said
Wait! There's something in my shoe.
so I said
No, I mean it, I've got to take it off.
then my brother said
No, I mean it. I've got to take it off.
so I said,
Hey! Stop copying me!
and he said
Hey! Stop copying me!
so I said
Stop copying me!
and he said
Stop copying me!
and we went on
Stop copying me!
Stop copying me!
Stop copying me!
Stop copying me!
Stop copying me!
Stop copying me!
Stop copying me!
Stop copying me!

till I yelled
STOOOOOOP IIIIIIIIIIITT
        NOOOOOOOOW!
right in his ear and he said
Ow.

THE SORT OF BOY

There's always the sort of boy
who has to get in first

who says he knows
whatever you know already,
he's known it for *ages*

who got whatever you just got
three weeks ago

or says there's a better one just out
and he's getting it with his Dad

who has to decide who's playing
and what they're going to play

and if it's Harry Potter,
he's always Harry Potter.

ANGLO-SAXON ME

My barrow's going to be awesome:
I'll be lying, propped up a bit,
on a comfortable sofa the size of a ship
that faces a TV almost as huge
and has a DVD with it and also a Wii;
all the remotes will be in easy reach,
and my DS, and lots of films and games,
and obviously a charger,
so none of the batteries run out
before I've finished travelling.

FREDDIE SPIDERS

At first he was just 'Freddie',
but then there was the day
the teacher saw a spider in the sink
and jumped for fear like a hiccup.

The rest of us jumped too,
and some of us backed away —
that spider was BIG —
but Freddie, loudmouth Freddie

walked quietly to the sink
and Freddie, fighting Freddie,
lifted the spider gently
like it was made of glass

then Freddie, who always runs,
walked quietly outside
and gently, carefully,
he set the spider down.

And that is why
we call him Freddie Spiders,
though Freddie says
the spiders call him 'Friend'.

EXCITED POEM

In four days it will be my birthday.
I'll get lots of presents from Mum and Dad.
All my friends'll come to my party:
we're going bowling and then we'll have cake.

In three days it will be my birthday.
I'll get lots of presents from Mum and Dad.
All my friends'll come to my party:
we're going birthday and then we'll have birthday.

In two days it will be my birthday.
I'll get lots of presents from Mum and Dad.
All my birthdays'll come to my birthday:
we're going birthday and then we'll have birthday.

In one day it will be my birthday.
I'll get lots of birthdays from Birthday and Birthday.
All my birthdays'll come to my birthday:
we're going birthday and then we'll have birthday.

Birthday birthday birthday birthday
Birthday birthday birthday birthday
Birthday birthday birthday birthday
Birthday birthday birthday YES!

JAKE AND MII

You know Jake in 4T? Well,
if he pushes me once more on purpose,
I'll switch the Wii on when I get home,
and I'll go to the Mii Channel
and I'll click on 'New Mii',
then 'Male', then 'Start from Scratch'
and make a tiny weedy body,
give it a head half-bald, the shape of brown toast
and eyes like cartoon bombs
with raggedy eyebrows,
a nose like a pair of apple pips,
a mouth the shape of dog mess,
a droopy moustache and big square specs,
then I'll make his top that stupid yellow
and call him Jake,
and then I'll hit 'Erase'.

THE DAY WE WENT TO THE MULTI-SKILLS FESTIVAL

jump skip
jump skip
jump skip
hop

throw catch
throw catch
throw catch
drop

dodge weave
dodge weave
dodge weave
bump

run chase
run chase
run chase
thump

trip fall
trip fall
trip fall
ow

toilet
toilet
toilet
now!

chatter
chatter
chatter
shhh!

your go
your go
YOUR GO!
push!

slurp chew
slurp chew
slurp chew
snack

trudge moan
trudge moan
trudge moan
back.

B-INSTRUCTIONS

I don't want bees on my birthday.
I don't want bricks in my bag.
I don't want bugs in my breakfast.
Just leave me alone and don't nag.

I won't touch the bumps in my bacon.
I won't use the bell on my bike.
I won't eat the black on bananas.
You don't understand what I like.

I can't get the boots on the baby.
I can't read the blurb on this book.
I can't see the boats for the bubbles.
I need you to help me to look.

And please: never butter my biscuits
or let brown bears sleep on my bed
and keep the bees out on my birthday.
I think we all know what I said.

THE PREFIX LESSON

Let's see if you've been listening.
Can you give me something that begins with 'anti-'?

Anti Julie lives in London.

Not quite what I was looking for.
Let's try another: 'un-'.

Un-cle Ian lives there too.

OK. Never mind. Have another go.
How about . . . 'pre-'?

Pre . . . tty soon they're coming to visit?

Oh dear. We'll try one more.
Now think carefully: 'dis-'

Dis . . . dis . . . . .
dis isn't going very well, is it?

COLLECT THEM ALL!

Series One! Out now!
Special features including
Arms! Legs! Heads! Feet! Tails!
Limited edition in all three dimensions
with detachable antennae!
Collect them all!

Series Two! Out yesterday!
Special features including
Fronts! Backs! Sides! Tops! Bottoms!
Limited edition in a full range of smells
with free extra nose-peg!
Collect them all!

Series Three! Out of sorts!
Special features including
Hiccups! Sneezes! Itches! Twitches! Dizzy spells!
Limited edition, exceptionally poorly,
with realistic snottynose!
Collect them all!

Series Four! Out and it doesn't care where!
Special features including
Sulks! Whines! Whinges! Moans and Mutterings!
Limited edition in a right old state
with its own box to shut it in.

Collect them all!

Series Five! Outside the law!
Special features including
Claws! Teeth! Venom! Stingers! Crushers!
Limited edition of fabulous nastiness
with secret evil plan.
Collect them all!

Collect them now!

Start collecting them!

OR ELSE.

FAMILY SWIMMING TIME

I think I might just watch today.
But you've got your costume on.

The water feels too cold.
But you've only put your toe in.

It's splashing on my face now.
So what? You're wearing goggles.

I don't like the big boys jumping in.
It's OK. We'll move away.

I think I might get out now.
You've only just got in.

Well don't leave me on my own!
But I want to have a swim.

I don't like it when I can't see you!
But I can swim — don't worry.

I know you can, but I can't!
Then just stay in the shallow end.

I don't like it in the water!
Mum, I know you don't, but you'll be fine.

NOT GOOD

It's boring, it's boring,
there's nothing to do.

It's rubbish, it's rubbish,
I want something new.

It's broken, it's broken,
it's stuck and it's slow.

It's stupid, it's stupid,
I don't want to go.

It's itchy, it's itchy,
I don't want to wear it.

It's your fault, it's your fault—
well, *I* didn't tear it.

He's silly, he's silly,
I don't want him here.

She's noisy, she's noisy,
she shouts in my ear.

It's yucky, it's yucky,
just take it away.

You're evil, you're evil,
I *hate* you today.

THE POTATOES MY DAD COOKS

Let me now praise the potatoes my Dad cooks
for truly they are epic;

for they come from the oven smelling so sweet,
their smell delights my nostrils

and when they sit steaming in their dish,
their crispy coatings delight my eyes

and when I take one up and bite it,
the coating breaks with a crunch

and when I chew that mouthful,
the mouthful delights my tongue

and then it delights my throat,
and then, oh then it warms my insides,

for truly the potatoes of my Dad are epic.
The potatoes of his enemies will fail.

MY FRIEND MICKEY

My friend Mickey was off school last week.
He was off for three whole days.
When I asked him why he just said *Ssshhh!*
I'll tell you breaktime.
Then at first break, he took my arm,
and he looked over his shoulder,
and he led me to the edge of the pitch,
the bit between the broken fence
and the pile of muddy leaves,
where he told me to *Get down!*
so I did, then he looked left and right
and he got down, and I asked *So?*
and he said *Well* . . . and he went *hmmm* . . .
so I said *Obviously, it's a secret.*
and he breathed out and said *I trust you.*
Truth is:
I've been in hiding.
In hiding? I asked. *Why?*
and he replied *Because I had a tip off.*
Headquarters said: lie low,
they're after you.
They know you did the job.
They traced the bullet to your nerf gun.
They know you're our best operative.
We need you safe. Stay down.
I nodded, then the bell went,

and Mickey coughed. A lot.
The enemy's poison gas, he said.

ROAR

We did a school show and I was a lion.
I was in one scene and I had one line
which was *Roar*,

but I made the best of my little part,
decided to take my one line — *Roar* —
and steal the scene with it,

so while I was waiting to go on with the others,
I clenched my teeth behind my mask
and I thought *Lion, lion, I'm a lion*, *Roar!*

and I curled my hands to claws and sprang
and I as I sprang I grew;
the *Roar* that came from my lungs was mighty,

so mighty it made the other kids jump
and all forget their lines,
so mighty it turned the grown-ups pale

and made the little children cry,
so mighty that it cracked the walls
and shook the plaster ceilings down

so mighty that the headteacher,
hair full of plaster, stood up
or tried to on the shaking floor

and told me to stop it, stop it
right there, or she'd have to stop the show
and I thought about eating her

but instead, I just left it at *Roar.*

THE TEACHER TELLS US HOW TO PLAY AT PLAYTIME

if someone's playing a game and you want to join them
ask nicely

if you're playing a game and someone wants to join you
then be kind

and even if there's really no room for them
say no nicely

if you want to join someone else's game and they say no
don't hit them

and if you've said no to someone and they've hit you
don't hit back

because the thing to do if someone's hit you
is telling me

and the thing to do if someone won't play with you
is asking someone else

because everyone here is everyone else's friend
and no buts

UNCLE SLAPPY AND AUNTIE BO

The strangest people you could know
were Uncle Slappy and Auntie Bo.
Mum used to visit when she was a kid—
I'm ever so happy that I never did.

They lived in a high-rise on floor 33,
the stairs took forever, the lift smelt of wee.
Kids had to leave hands and feet at the door,
so as not to mess Auntie Bo's walls or her floor.

You can't really play with no hands and no feet,
so all Mum could do was sit still on a seat
and talk to her cousins, who were very quiet.
She thinks that was something to do with their diet—

well, if fishbones and gruel were all you ever got,
would you feel like talking? I'd have to say not.
Sometimes, in a specially generous mood,
Bo would give one kid a tin of cat food.

It didn't come free though: that tin was a prize
for being the toughest kid in that high-rise.
They played High Rise Bounce, and in order to win
and get sole chomping rights on the meat in that tin

they'd jump out the window, and then, oh my gosh,
the kid who bounced highest got given the nosh.
Mum said it was terrible, hearing the groans
as Slappy and Bo did their rounds, setting bones,

and the winnings, well they were no more than a token:
you can't spoon much up when your fingers are broken.
They said Mum could play, but she never joined in:
she said it looked horrid, the stuff in that tin.

She's funny, my Mum: when I asked for a look
at some snaps of them all in a photograph book
she said that she'd lost them — although they took dozens;
what's more, she'd completely lost touch with her cousins.

NEW BABY IN OUR HOUSE

Yesterday, while I was at school,
Mum brought the new baby home
in a travelling basket.
When I got back, the baby was hiding
behind the sofa. All I could see were eyes.
But then I wiggled my fingers
and the baby came forward,
one paw at a time, and I said,
'*Good* boy! Come on! Come on!'
and the baby sniffed my fingers;
then I dragged them back, very slowly
so the baby followed them out,
and after that it was great — me and the baby
played for hours, and me and the baby —
wait! Do I mean 'kitten'?

OUR CLASS: AN ABC

A is for Asha, who talks when she shouldn't.

B is for Ben, who shrugs in reply.

C is for Carrie, cherished and only.

D is for Daniel, the youngest of nine.

E is for Emily, who won't put her hand up.

F is for Fergus, who knows all the answers.

G is for Gemma, who can do the splits.

H is for Harry, who can't kick a ball straight.

I is for Isabel, whose writing's the neatest.

J is for Jessica, who can't make the letters join.

K is for Khalil, working at the speed of light.

L is for Lottie, still sounding the words out.

M is for Marcus, shouting and barging.

N is for Niamh, who's everyone's mum.

O is for Ollie, small but clever.

P is for Pippa, also clever but very tall.

Q is for Quinn, who hates the uniform for not
being pink.

R is for Ryan, who hates pink.

S is for Sam, who does what the others do.

T is for Thomas, who tells them what's what.

U is for Una, with big sisters, who knows all the
cool stuff.

V is for Vicky, who couldn't care less.

W is for William, who's always the captain.

X is for Xander, who's always in goal.

Y is for Yalaina, who also plays football.

And Z is for Zack, who was born with his own
drum, and dances to it.

THE TOTEM POLE IN THE MUSEUM

Carved red wood
14 metres high,
it came in
through a hole
in the floor,
and even now
it nearly touches
the glass roof.
An eagle perches
on the top,
resting its feet
on a thunderbird
that stands on
a killer whale
with a blowhole
and under that
is the face
of a man
and under him
there's a beaver
at the bottom.
If you stand
on the floor
behind the beaver

and look up,
you can see
the eagle's bum.

EASTER EGGS

Sadie opened her Easter egg
and found three smaller Easter eggs.

Jaspar opened his Easter egg
and found a hammer for breaking Easter eggs.

Monica opened her Easter egg
and found a tiny doll she thought she'd lost.

Stephen opened his Easter egg
and found last week's uneaten peas.

Naomi opened her Easter egg
and found the answers to next week's Maths test.

Oscar opened his Easter egg,
put one half to his ear and heard the peeping of
newborn chicks.

Sonya opened her Easter egg,
walked inside and no-one saw her till the
following year

when Anton opened his Easter egg
and Sonya jumped out.

NOTHINGNESS

The worst thing
about playing on your own
is you sometimes catch
the sound of nothingness

and I'm telling you,
there is no sound so scary,

so what you have to do
is turn on the TV
or the computer or the Wiii
or your DS

or turn them all right up
or think of a reason to call your Mum
or else you could just sing it away
like this: *Laladidoooooooooooooooo*

I LIKE TO WATCH PEOPLE FALL OVER

There's a show on and it's my favourite,
the best thing on Freeview TV,
where you get to watch people fall over:
it's the funniest thing you could see.

Sometimes they're children and babies,
sometimes they're women and men
but whoever they are they fall over
again and again and again.

The athlete trips over the hurdle,
the bride always lands in the cake
and then someone famous falls over
in take after take after take.

Never mind that it's grey and it's raining
and nobody's come round to play,
if I get to watch people fall over,
I call that a brilliant day.

So keep all your silly knock-knock jokes
and don't bother pulling that face,
just go and trip up and fall over
and I'll fall about the place.

AWESOME AND RANDOM

I have two friends, Random and Awesome
who always play with me.
'LOL!' says Random.
Says Awesome, 'OMG!'

At breaktime, with Random and Awesome,
we always miss the bell.
'OMG!' cries Awesome.
Cries Random, 'LOL!'

When they come round, Awesome and Random,
I say we'll have sharkmeat for tea.
'LOL!' says Random.
Says Awesome, 'OMG!'

That's the thing about Random and Awesome:
they love the jokes I tell.
'OMG!' says Awesome,
and Random, 'LOL!'

But sometimes with Awesome and Random,
I'll hurt myself, and wail.
Then Random will say 'Awwwkwaaard.'
and Awesome, 'Epic Fail!'

BUTTERFLY AND CROCODILE

At swimming once,
I went to turn from front to back
and just kept turning,
just kept turning,
turning over,
over and over,
till the swimming teacher said,
'What are you doing?'
and I said, 'I'm a crocodile.
This is the death roll
that crocodiles do
to tear their prey apart.'

'OK', she said,
'You need to work on your butterfly now —
though I must say
your crocodile
is really coming on.'

A DIFFERENCE OF OPINION

I said, if the universe ended, then everything would
 be white,
because white is the colour of nothing.

Mum said no, if there was nothing it would be no
 colour,
because a colour needs a something.

I said she didn't understand, she wasn't listening
and that white *was* no colour.

She said she did understand, she was listening
and that white was *a* colour.

I said she was being a stupid idiot,
and that it was all right to say so.

She said she was not being a stupid idiot,
and that it was not all right to call her that.

I said I was still getting my pocket money anyway.

She said I wasn't.

I said I was sorry.

She said OK.

DIFFERENT WISHING

I wish I had a little brother.
I wish I didn't have a little brother.

I'd have someone to play with.
There'd be no-one to get on my nerves.

We could make stuff together.
I could make stuff and leave it out and no-one would break it.

I'd have someone to talk to.
There wouldn't be this voice all the time going nyah nyah nyah.

We could watch TV together.
I wouldn't have to fight over the remote.

I could explain things to them.
I wouldn't have to answer stupid questions all day.

We could have sleepovers every night.
I could go to sleep in peace.

Mum and Dad would have someone else to nag.
Mum and Dad would spend twice as much money on me.

I wish they'd asked me if I wanted one.
I wish they'd asked me if I didn't.

WHAT I FOUND UNDER MY BED

Tattered comics, broken cars
    wrappers off old chocolate bars.

Single slippers, lonely socks,
    half a chess set in a box.

A month of dust, a year of fluff,
    some other damper, dirty stuff.

Stuff that bored me, stuff I hid
    and all the reasons why I did.

Forgotten facts of other sorts,
    a heap of interrupted thoughts.

A crumpled length of paper chain,
    a dream I'll never have again.

Cracker crumbs and pencil ends,
    three lost imaginary friends.

THERE WAS A WIND . . .

There was a wind and it was a big wind
and it blew my mother's hat away

There was a wind and it was a big wind
it turned umbrellas inside out
and it blew my mother's hat away

There was a wind and it was a big wind
it made the crows fly backwards
it turned umbrellas inside out
and it blew my mother's hat away

There was a wind and it was a big wind
it ripped the branches off the trees
it made the crows fly backwards
it turned umbrellas inside out
and it blew my mother's hat away

There was a wind and it was a big wind
it punched five people off their bicycles
it ripped the branches off the trees
it made the crows fly backwards
it turned umbrellas inside out
and it blew my mother's hat away

There was a wind and it was a big wind
it shoved a hatchback sideways
it punched five people off their bicycles
it ripped the branches off the trees
it made the crows fly backwards
it turned umbrellas inside out
and it blew my mother's hat away

There was a wind and it was a big wind
it stirred up the sky like a spoon in soup
it shoved a hatchback sideways
it punched five people off their bicycles
it ripped the branches off the trees
it made the crows fly backwards
it turned umbrellas inside out
and it blew my mother's hat away

There was a wind and it was a big wind
it moved all the wheelie bins to riot
it stirred up the sky like a spoon in soup
it shoved a hatchback sideways
it punched five people off their bicycles
it ripped the branches off the trees
it made the crows fly backwards
it turned umbrellas inside out
and it blew my mother's hat away

There was a wind and it was a big wind
it pushed over signposts and knocked down poles
it moved all the wheelie bins to riot
it stirred up the sky like a spoon in soup
it shoved a hatchback sideways
it punched five people off their bicycles
it ripped the branches off the trees
it made the crows fly backwards
it turned umbrellas inside out
and it blew my mother's hat away

There was a wind and it was a big wind
it sheared the roof off the local school
it pushed over signposts and knocked down poles
it moved all the wheelie bins to riot
it stirred up the sky like a spoon in soup
it shoved a hatchback sideways
it punched five people off their bicycles
it ripped the branches off the trees
it made the crows fly backwards
it turned umbrellas inside out
and it blew my mother's hat away

and we looked at it all
the flapping roof and the broken signposts
the rioting bins and the churning sky
the dented car and the riderless bikes
the naked trees and the dizzy crows
the broken umbrellas and the hat,

my mother's hat, flying over the chimney tops
and there was nothing, nothing we could say:
the wind had taken our words away.

LOST

I lost my temper once
and then when I looked round
I found I'd lost my Golden Time.

The teacher sent my Mum a note;
then she sent me to the Lost Time Room
to look, but instead I lost my way

and wound up in Lost Property
with shoes that lost their partners
and hats that lost their heads.

I nearly lost heart then
but I took some good advice
and tried again,

turned left instead of right;
I pushed a different door
and there it was: my Golden Time,

a puppyish sort of thing,
running up to meet me
with my temper in its mouth.

THE END

Once the sun is gone,
the earth will have nothing to orbit around

so it will go further and further away,
getting colder and colder and colder

till everyone's dead,
then eventually

it'll reach a black hole — it's *bound* to —
and get sucked in.